And in Love

MW01180890

2020
We need each other!
Say it, show it, live it
EVERYDAY

♡ Joan

April — 2021
Bob & Joyce —
what an amazing
connection!

♡ Joan

Joan Cogan

outskirts
press

Once a teacher / Still a teacher / Always a teacher

I entered her classroom in 1964 as a cocky 15 year old. I exited as a future Ohio State Buckeye, ready to succeed in college. Mrs. Anderson never measured my worth by a letter grade. She only saw my strengths and potential. Her welcoming attitude was uplifting and contagious. She was glad to be in the classroom and so was I. She helped me understand the roadblocks that got in my way were merely temporary agents of growth. She believed in me. She embraced me then. She embraces me now. For fifty-flve years Mrs. Anderson has been in, out, and back in my life, just a telephone call away. That, my friends, is the power of an exceptional engaged teacher! I am proud to dedicate my book to the one who empowered me to tell my story, Mrs. Anderson. Yes, I am indeed grateful to be anchored in her love.

Once a teacher / Still a teacher / Always a teacher

PLEASE COME

I am excited you are holding this book. I am happy you are willing to walk with me. The title on the cover might have peaked your curiosity. Perhaps someone purchased it for you because they were also interested. What is a LAND ANCHOR and why is it so important anyway? I need my land anchors and so do you. The difference is you might not know it yet. I'm more than five decades older and learned from many mistakes. I dedicate my story to you. You matter! Consider each letter in the word ANCHOR and **come with me.**

THINK A:

- approachable and accepting
- affirming and authentic

An anchor will acknowledge you as is, not attempt to fix you. An anchor knows you are not broken, but perhaps you need an ally.

THINK N:

- nice and nourishing
- nimble and nifty

An anchor is nurturing. You know you are cared for no matter how flawed you think you may be. An anchor offers newness, a fresh idea. It is not the routine or possibly a rut you may be experiencing.

THINK C:

- calm and comfortable
- connection and clarity

An anchor knows how and when to communicate with you, but won't pry. An anchor is committed to walk with you, yes you, no matter what the circumstances.

THINK H:

- honest and hopeful
- humble and humorous

An anchor always extends a helping hand to you. An anchor believes in hard work, relentless energy to make your situation bearable.

THINK O:

- opportunity and organization
- optimistic and open

An anchor is observant. He is quick to notice when you are in danger, emotional danger that is. An anchor is outfitted to assist and protect you through the power of words.

THINK R:

- resilient and respectful
- responsible and reliable

An anchor wants a relationship with you. An anchor will reinforce all that is good in you.

You matter! Please come with me as we gather specific information about the **POWER** of a Land Anchor. Problem solving **together** will be less painful. Open the door! Walking wounded is **not** healthy. I pose several questions only you can answer. I trust you will answer each one honestly. Are you experiencing any guilt or shame? Before you answer remember they are not the same thing. Guilt is knowing *you did* something bad. Shame is *you are* bad. Are you feeling like you do not or can never measure up to what others expect? It may be in the classroom or a situation in your home. Is it your relationship with others? No doubt siblings, peers, teachers, parents, coaches, or neighborhood drama are often exhausting. I get tired just thinking about it at age 70. Is your mind cluttered with uncertainty? Is your stress level demanding, challenging, or threatening your physical and/or mental health? Do you know your triggers? Stress can motivate you or it can flatten you like a pancake. If you spot danger ahead do you act or curl up in a ball?

Stress can be brutal and overwhelming. Instead of chaos and confusion I want you to **SEEK CALM**. You will be better when you discover your land anchor. Your land anchor just may even find you. You must, I repeat, MUST, let that land anchor into your life. You matter! Open the door. Welcome your guest. I hope your internal dialogue sounds something like this "I am really glad you are here. I am thrilled you came. I am ready to get started on our trip. Thanks for inviting me to walk with you."

Let's meet B.J., your stabilizer, your imaginary friend, your much needed Land Anchor.

WHAT is a Land Anchor? You need to know what you are looking for before you can find it. Is it the quarterback leading the offense down the football field? Is it the store in the mall that lures customers into the parking lot? Is it the fastest man in a relay race to receive the baton? Is it the last, most likely, strongest, at the end of the rope in a game of tug of war? Yes, these may be anchors, but I'm talking about B.J., your imaginary friend. He cares about you. His presence provides comfort, security, and relief. B.J. is strong, reliable, and supportive. He embraces you "as is." He acts as your emotional **compass**. As he gets to know you, he will help you when nothing else seems to be working. Our internal dialogue might sound like this "I am out of sync. I am wrongly judged by my peers, adults too, because I come from a broken home. I didn't make the choir. My grades are never good enough. I stink at sports." The negative talk will intensify if it is not shared, or at least acknowledged. You know without a doubt you are heading towards danger. Let that **compass**, your land anchor, walk with you in a safer direction.

THINK and REFLECT:
What is a warning sign that you need a land anchor?

_____

_____

_____

_____

_____

_____

What will your land anchor do to help you?

_____

_____

_____

_____

_____

What can you do to redirect your thinking?

_____

_____

_____

_____

_____

WHAT B.J. offers to you is a clearer, maybe totally different perspective. In the trenches of confusion your vision is certainly blurry. B.J. is an ally with **acute timing**. I call him sharp-minded. He appears to be one with eyes in the back of his head. Keep the door open! Continue to walk with him. He matters! You matter!

Who is your Land Anchor, your imaginary B.J.? It is not about age, gender, grade point average, athletic ability, or physical appearance. B.J. is inclusive, open, and stays connected. He is genuine, authentic, and cares about you. Yes YOU! As you experience challenges and obstacles that just don't add up you will not be judged by B.J. Much like my land anchors B.J. will listen, not just with his ears, but with his heart. He will hear your pain and not attempt to fix you. Instead he will walk with you. He will carry you when it is necessary. He will sense uncertainty, turmoil, and a host of pressures. He will act on your behalf, but knows you must do the work. He will not enable. You have choices. You, not him, must be the final decision maker. You matter! You matter to B.J.

THINK and REFLECT:
Who are you willing to share that unpleasant in the gut stuff with now? Yes, now!

_____

_____

_____

_____

_____

_____

Name a painful situation that is paralyzing you mentally and/or emotionally. Yes, now!

_____

_____

_____

_____

_____

_____

How might your internal dialogue change once that helpless, maybe hopeless feeling is shared? Remember B.J. will not abandon you.

_____

_____

_____

_____

_____

_____

WHO: The Terrific Trio, my forever present land anchors

- Rose Anderson - my inspiring high school history teacher
- Vicky Moore - the amazing mom of two of my former students, Jason and Ryan
- Cindy Klingensmith - my trusted colleague that enjoyed sixth grade camp as much as I did

A SCHOOL CONNECTION

Rose was stuck with me because I was on her class list. Vicky was stuck with me too because years ago parents did not even think about requesting a teacher for their child. Cindy was hired to fill the sixth grade position. She did not have a choice either.

THE COMMON THREAD

For the past thirty, forty, even fifty years I have been anchored by Rose, Vicky, and Cindy. For many reasons I have been in, out, and back in their lives. They are etched in my emotional memory bank. Now it is my time to think and reflect.

The Terrific Trio

- a constant, a link to clarity
- plants an optimistic voice in my head
- picks me up and dusts me off when I stumble
- provides a vision, a mental picture, when I am looking at a blank screen

I want the **WHO** in your life to be as powerful as mine. When you are tense, uneasy, uncomfortable, possibly coming unglued, I want you to be prepared. Risky behavior and addiction is not the answer. I'm hoping you will find that land anchor. I'm hoping he may even find you. You matter! You matter to him! You matter to me!

WHEN

You will surely know **When** you need B.J., your imaginary land anchor. Your life is spinning completely out of control. The time is **NOW**, not later. There is no GREAT ESCAPE. You may run from your reality, but it will find you. You cannot hide. At times I found myself drifting aimlessly from the shore. Heaps of relentless wind kept pushing me into deeper water. Before long my feet could not touch the bottom. In desperation I searched for a buoy, a lifeline, anything to keep me afloat. At age 15 I had no knowledge of coping skills. Out of nowhere I heard shouting. "Focus, begin treading water." That I could do. "Focus, lie on your back, use your feet, listen to your body, just float, just float." That my friends is your land anchor, speaking on your behalf, empowering you to do the work. You matter!

THINK and REFLECT:

When do you know you are emotionally drifting? Describe the situation.

_____

_____

_____

_____

_____

_____

What message is your internal dialogue sending you?

_____

_____

_____

_____

_____

_____

How can B.J. redirect your thinking?

_____

_____

_____

_____

_____

_____

WHEN do you know that B.J., your imaginary land anchor, is working?

Consider This!

- when you are able to love more and fear less
- when you are able to grow and live in the present not regret your past mistakes
- when you take each day as it comes and make it the best you can

- when you own your shortcomings, work on correction, but refuse to beat yourself up because of them
- when you act kinder, more gentle, and even begin to cherish who you are becoming

Much like you, I am a work in progress. The terrific trio is right by my side, a telephone call away. This is what I want for you. Continue to know when to reach out. Your land anchor is not a mind reader, but will remain a constant ally. Keep them in your life. You matter to them!

WHERE

Where will you find B.J., your imaginary land anchor? Searching for him on the computer is a risky gamble, a game of chance. Please don't take it. Be willing to reach out, even when you don't feel like it. Introduce yourself. Move away from, maybe out of your comfort zone. Don't spend valuable time tweeting. Limit the use of Facebook, LinkedIn, and Instagram.

Think and decide to **choose where** you will find an emotional connection. Discovering Rose, Vicky, and Cindy, my land anchors, occurred in the classroom. **Where** do you spend most of your time? Perhaps a school building is an ideal place for you to search. It may be a special teacher, a coach, a cook, a custodian, an upperclassman, a hall monitor. **Where** do extracurricular activities take place? Can you begin relationships with anyone there? Even though you think you are alone and you may be right, you are **NOT**. Someone, some**where** is looking for you! It is a place you **must** explore or continue to walk wounded. If not school, is your neighborhood a possibility? Volunteering to help others is a great way to get acquainted. It certainly was for me. I understand times have changed, but people have not. Snow needs shoveled, leaves need raked, plants need watered, grass needs mowed. Think of your lonely and/or elderly neighbors. Could you spend ten minutes a couple times a week with them or possibly run an errand? If you DO GOOD you will begin to FEEL GOOD, if **not** good maybe just a little better.

THINK and REFLECT:

Is technology improving or ruining your relationships?

_____

_____

_____

_____

_____

_____

How much screen time is just right for you? How do you know?

_____

_____

_____

_____

_____

_____

WHERE you spend your time is critical. Building relationships and connecting emotionally is healthy. A personal touch, not an emoji is what I want for you. You matter! Yes, you matter!

Why do you need a land anchor? Why is B.J., your imaginary friend, lurking in your mind? Brain research confirms that risk taking spikes during adolescence. Turmoil and uncertainty leads to danger. Who am I? Where do I fit in? Confusion often results in:

- alcohol/tobacco abuse
- over the counter pill popping
- illegal street drugs
- unsafe sex
- eating disorders
- acts of violence
- cutting/self-harm

Reach out! Find that compass!

Addiction and/or suicidal thoughts are possibly in your internal dialogue. B.J. senses the urgency to offer you clarity. He leads you to understand that you may be bent, but not broken. What you are experiencing is real, but not permanent. B.J. will take that emotional roller coaster ride with you. He acknowledges your highs, lows, tight turns, and steep slopes. He accepts your disappointment, unhappiness, and at times desperation. Remember B.J. is patient, models resilience, and believes in you.

THINK and REFLECT:

What risky behavior is luring you in? Are you going to take the bait?

_____

_____

_____

_____

_____

_____

How are your peers influencing your decision making?

_____

_____

_____

_____

_____

What is your internal dialogue saying regarding the consequences of your behavior?

_____

_____

_____

_____

_____

_____

WHY - Those stomach-churning experiences of adolescence can be emotionally paralyzing. Embrace every opportunity to lean in, not away from B.J. He is keeping you grounded. You need him in your life. He cares about you. I care about you. You matter!

A ROADBLOCK

Whoa! What happened to my stepping stone? B.J., your imaginary friend, begins to explain. This is an emotional obstacle. It is placed across our path for halting or perhaps hindering our progress. Think of a fallen tree in the middle of the road. How do you manage to maneuver around it? Keep in mind a roadblock is a problem, not an issue. A problem is a situation that needs resolved. There is an answer. An issue is a topic that is discussed. It is often debated.

ROADBLOCK 1:

FEAR OF FAILURE - Is that keeping you from moving forward? Being afraid is brutal and quite overwhelming.

- fear of a bad grade
- fear of not fitting in
- fear of going to summer camp, any overnighter alone
- fear of the unknown or uncharted territory

Listen to B.J.'s suggestions:

* Find a way to benefit from your past mistakes. Thomas Alva Edison said; "I have not failed. I've just found 10,000 ways that won't work." Chances are if you don't learn from your mistakes you will repeat them. It's difficult to find a silver lining, but there just might be one. Keep your eyes open. Stay focused.

* When failure is possible, can you view it as a challenge? Do you remember the story of *The Little Engine That Could*? Many times he must stop, look fear in the face, and repeat, "I think I can, I think I can, I think I can."

* Be kind to yourself when you experience failure. Emotional pain accelerates during adolescence. Remember you are under construction, a work in progress, not a finished project.

ROADBLOCK 2:

DRIVE TO SUCCEED - What is propelling you to think that you must always be number one? This, like fear, can be emotionally dangerous and damaging. You cannot move forward because you have **NO** balance and that is not an issue. It is a problem and you must OWN it.

Listen to B.J.'s suggestions:

* Find a way to rest and relax. If you don't know how I'll help you. Block out 20 minutes, same time, every day for you, just you. Set a timer so it becomes a habit. Rest and relax. It can be as simple as a call to a friend, a walk with a neighbor, listening to music, soaking in the tub. Whatever works, just do it.

* Stop comparing yourself to others. It is blocking the vision of yourself. You must let go or jealously wins. Do not let the achievements, advantages, or

possessions of others define you. Concentrate solely on doing and being your own personal best.

* Erase the thought of compromising your values to be that number one. Don't let your drive be so intense that you cheat to get what you want. You are not only cheating yourself, but cheating others as well.

CRITICAL REMINDER - Roadblocks are temporary, not permanent. They are problems, not issues. I'm ready to continue walking, even if we take an alternate route. Let's go.

Whatever roadblock you are facing, B.J., your imaginary anchor, will not leave you. He is a stabilizer, but not an enabler. You MUST make a choice. Are you willing to do the work? A roadblock is an effective way to alert a walker of danger. The situation is no longer safe. The process of moving forward, taking ownership, is entirely up to you.

How do you get from point A to point B safely?

THINK and DECIDE:
What kind of bone are you right now, today?

The Wishbone spends most of his time wishing the roadblock would disappear. He has a strong desire for something positive to happen, but chooses to do nothing.

The Jawbone uses his mouth only. The roadblock is still impeding his progress. He just talks, idle chatter, nonstop - on and on and on. There is absolutely no chance of anything changing.

The Knucklebone mocks others. He is skilled at insulting, humiliating, and intimidating. The roadblock is always someone else's fault, not his. He too goes nowhere.

The Backbone demonstrates strength, strength of character. He refuses to allow the roadblock to defeat him. He does not waiver or surrender. He instead commits himself to the hard work ahead. The roadblock begins to propel him in a different direction.

How do you get from point A to point B safely? I'm glad you decided to follow the example of the **Backbone**.

HOW - Have you ever heard this phrase? "When the going gets tough, the tough get going." I bet your grandparents know exactly what it means. PUSH! PUSH! <u>P</u>ush <u>U</u>ntil <u>S</u>omething <u>H</u>appens! Natural consequences are out of your control. Chances are it is **not** what you expected. THAT'S LIFE! A dreadful situation is getting uglier by the minute. **How** do you accept what happened? You must have a back-up plan, maybe even two. You are forced to choose a different direction, an alternate route. That's life!

THINK and REFLECT:
Describe a specific activity that you expected to happen at home or school. It never did. What did you do about the situation? Did you have a back up plan? Is there anything you could have done?

_____

_____

_____

_____

_____

_____

THINK NATURAL CONSEQUENCES
Describe an event in your life that was out of your control. Explain how you responded.

_____
_____
_____
_____
_____
_____

THAT`S LIFE.
Name one thing you simply had to accept.

_____
_____
_____
_____
_____
_____

CRITICAL REMINDER: You are not alone. B.J. will walk with you. You may be bent, but you are not broken. Share that emotional pain. Get that roadblock out of your way! You matter!

PLEASE STAY

I am glad you came, opened the door, and walked each stepping stone with me. My hope is that you took time and answered each question in the book. If you didn't, do it now. Yes, now. If you are willing to write your thoughts then and only then do you truly **OWN** them. Think about your Internal Dialogue. Were you truthful? Reread your responses. The most powerful tool you **OWN** is what you repeatedly tell yourself. It is your ID without showing a card. The terrific trio, Rose, Vicky, and Cindy, believed in me. They were NOT connected to my insecurities and negative self-talk. They **ONLY** saw potential. Try seeing yourself through the eyes of B.J., your imaginary land anchor. He will give you a sense of belonging. He will stay. You see, this is **NOT** the end of the story, but just the beginning.

THINK and REFLECT:
Life is a choice. What does "play the cards you are dealt" mean?

_____

_____

_____

_____

_____

_____

Honesty is not the best policy. It is the **only** policy. How does this affect your ability to build lasting healthy relationships?

_____

_____

_____

_____

_____

_____

Emotional agility is being comfortable in your **own** skin. How confident are you today, right now?

_____

_____

_____

_____

_____

_____

THE POWER of WORDS

Turn up the volume to good words in your head. Send a signal to your heart to hear the same thing. Every word you speak, every action you take, and every deed you perform, sends a message. What does your message say? Words do paint your reality. Listen carefully. Choose your words wisely.

RETHINK ROADBLOCKS and RISKY BEHAVIORS

A roadblock stops progression. It is like running on a treadmill going absolutely nowhere. This is the time destructive behavior rears its ugly head. You may feel detached, cut off from others, leading you to alcohol, drug abuse and self -harm. **Reminder**: A roadblock is temporary. You will find a way to maneuver around it or maybe through it with B.J. by your side. He has empowered you to keep moving. There is no reset button. There is no looking back, only forward. B.J. is staying.

OUR MENTAL MAPS

A mental map is a self perception. You carry it around in your head. You use it everyday. The terrific trio, Rose, Vicky, and Cindy, always gave me a clearer mental map of myself. I was bent, but not broken. I opened the door, let them in, leaned on them for strength and direction when I had very little of my own. Guess what? They stayed! Where is your mental map taking you? Are you thinking about walking with a land anchor?

THE FINAL CHALLENGE

- Continue to seek that land anchor. I'm thankful the terrific trio chose to stay. Gratitude is a warm feeling to hold in your heart.
- Believe and trust that your land anchor will walk with you during the good, the bad, and the ugly times.

- Love yourself today, even though you're not sure exactly how.
- Forgive yourself and others too, even when you much rather not.
- Envision a chunk of good happening to you each day.
- Offer the best of who you are right now to others.
- Embrace the positives surrounding you. I avoid naysayers as much as possible.
- Recall all things worth being. I want you to see the value in you. You matter! You matter to me! Yes, You!

In my imaginary neighborhood you live right next door. I`m thankful we shared this incredible time together.

ANCHORED in GRATITUDE,

Joan

YOU MATTER

I APPRECIATE YOU!

- the KEY BOARD POUNDER, Katie Pettigrew, who managed to turn my chicken scratch into a typed manuscript
- the PAPARAZZI, Laurie Traganza, who armed with camera awaited a call for a photo shoot
- the entire OUTSKIRTS PRESS crew who made the publication of my story a reality

WHO ELSE MATTERS?

THE COGAN CLAN

- nephews, John, Jeff and Dan, who captured the hearts of their wives, Kennedy, Deb and Sneha
- nieces, Julie and Katie who secured husbands, Josh and Mike that loved strong willed women
- the dream team of 8 great nieces, Ellie, Lucy, Anna, Harper, Hadley, Harlow, Ady, Jiya and 1 great nephew, Everett, who own a huge chunk of my happiness
- cousin Vaughn and wife Susan, who I thought was a librarian, but later discovered she stayed home and read to her daughters

THE COMMUNITY of Northwest Local School District

- to the many students who bragged - "We have blue smart puddles on our cement classroom floor, and you don't."
- to the parents who pleaded - "I won't believe anything I've heard about you if you don't believe anything you've heard about my kid."
- to the administrative team who held their breath when answering a call - "What has Cogan done now?"
- to the countless colleagues who wondered – "What can she possibly think of next?"
- to the entire village that values emotional welfare and academics as its highest priority
- to the soon to be YMCA, a great place to continue building relationships that matter

Whatever stepping stone you are standing on, please keep moving forward, one day at a time.

Anchored in Love,
Joan

CPSIA information can be obtained
at www.ICGtesting.com
Printed in the USA
FFHW021018040120
57496025-62926FF